THE
SUSTAINABLE
CHEF

Andy Oakey

First paperback edition published December 2021

Printed on FSC® certified paper by youloveprint
– a CarbonNeutral® certified production company

Book design by Andy Oakey
Recipes by Andy Oakey
Photos by Andy Oakey, Julian Oakey, Pippa Oakey

ISBN 978-1-80068-429-4 (paperback)

www.sustainablechef.net

Dedicated to my Mum, who taught me how to cook many years ago and always likes to experiment with recipes. Mum likes cooking!

CONTENTS

PREFACE

It is undeniable that the world is facing a climate crisis. Human activity has accelerated the natural changes in our climate, leaving many people wondering what they can do to help. One potential answer lies in the often-overlooked area of food and diet.

This book gives you a wide selection of recipes, both sweet and savoury, to help you reduce your climate impact from food. Every recipe is 100% plant-based if it is followed to the word, meaning that the associated emissions are generally much lower than their animal-based counterparts.

Now, I am not a perfect vegan – far from it in fact; but I do try to eat plant-based where I can to help reduce my personal contribution to emissions. So, if you fancy the occasional milk chocolate bar or a friend has cooked a non-plant based meal for you, then go ahead and enjoy them. Equally, if you are new to not eating the traditional 'meat and 2-veg' every day then perhaps start small with one day-a-week (e.g. meat-free Mondays) and build from there.

The world's problems won't be solved by a select few taking complete responsibility, but if we all chip in, make a few small changes, and share the burden, there is still hope we can tackle what's ahead.

HOW TO USE THIS BOOK

This book has been written with a desire to minimise the challenges and confusion faced by many other recipes; making sustainable cooking and baking less daunting.

Naturally, this is still a cookbook so you need to be prepared to get stuck in, but hopefully some of the features of this book can help you along the way.

These icons tell you how long each recipe should take, how many servings, and any storage points.

Each recipe is presented with no-nonsense instructions with the key points highlighted so you can't miss them.

Look out for top tips which may help with anything difficult, or perhaps give a slight twist on a recipe.

Everyone like their own way of doing things, and you shouldn't be afraid to experiment. Drop any notes in here.

The carbon impact check shows you how good this recipe is compared to a 'typical' popular equivalent. If you're interested in the science/ maths beind this then check out page 108.

EQUIPMENT & TOOLS

Much like clever DIY gizmos, cooking and baking is made easier by fancy gadgets and cookware but are definitely **NOT** essential. Having just a few basics all you need to be able to make some delicious creations, plus it is significantly cheaper and takes up less room in your kitchen.

I am, however, an advocate of **quality** equipment... I bet that £10 set of pots and pans you once bought after moving out didn't last very long! Finding the balance is tricky, but I generally find that equipment from the own-brand (non-basics!) section in supermakets is about the right level.

You should be able to make every recipe in this book with the following:
1) Large frying pan – preferably about 10cm deep
2) A couple of saucepans of different sizes
3) Large Square Tin
4) 2x Round Cake Tins
5) Loaf Tin
6) Flat Baking Tray/Sheet
7) 12-Hole Muffin Tin
8) Ramekins
9) Pie-£in – loose bottom if possible
10) Cake cases – resuable if possible
11) Greaseproof paper/liners – reusable if possible
12) Grater
13) Mixing bowls
14) Knives, Spoons, Spatulas, and a Masher
15) Oven-Proof Dish
16) Scales
17) Blender
18) Electric hand mixer (optional, but makes some jobs a lot faster and easier)

Of course, if you have other fancy gadgets, then by all means use them. If you want to get something gadgety, then my first suggestion is an electric hand mixer – it is very affordable compared to many items (~£10), and can be used in many recipes.

METHOD & INGREDIENT TIPS

At some point when cooking, you will have the classic moment when you realise you don't have enough of something for the recipe, or perhaps you don't have the right tin.

This is not a problem – 95% of the time you can work around this; let me show you...

"My recipe needs a 20cm square tin but mine is only 18cm."

Simple enough, either use the full recipe and put any excess into another tin/cake cases, or multiply the ingredients by about 80%. Remember that if you multiply a cake recipe, you work to the area of the tin, not just one dimension.

"I don't have enough demarara sugar... I'm 10g short!"

Another easy one – think about how much sugar the recipe wants overall and you can decide based on that. If you are 10g short when you need 50g then you will need to find a substitute for that 10g (see below), but 10g when it is saying 200g isn't going to make much difference; substitute or just leave it out.

"I need red kidney beans but only have pinto beans... is that ok?"

If you have something similar then by all means substitute. The closer the substitute, the better – particularly when making something like Sticky Toffee Pudding, where the flavour comes form the sugar. Often you can swap quite different items and find you have a new creation, e.g. perhaps you don't have spinach for the quiche recipe – try using another leafy green vegetable or even a different vegetable altogether.

Don't be afraid to test things, particularly where flavours are concerned. The main swap I would not make is between Baking Powder and Bicarbonate of Soda... they work differently to each other so could have some disappointing results.

Also a common question is **"Is my oven a fan oven or not?"**. The majority of modern ovens are fan forced, but not all ovens are equal. My worn out fan oven means I set it a little hotter. Test different levels to get to know your own!

METHOD & INGREDIENT TIPS

In terms of the ingredients themselves, there are a few things to be aware of...

Sugars: A lot of the time, these can be interchanged and there will only be a slight change in flavour; however, I would be wary of swapping out dark brown or demarara sugar as they are usually used for a specific flavour.

Flours: The recipes in this book only use plain flour. This is because self-raising can vary between brands and can loose its raising strength.

Oils and Fats: A variety are used in this book. Vegetable oil can be swapped for sunflower and often olive oils. Plant-based spreads can be used in many recipes, but wherever you see "Not Spread", this means you need to use a block butter (typically these can be plant-based too), or the end result may not be so good.

Nutritional Yeast: A plant-based product giving a cheesy flavour. Find it in the free-from or sauces section in most supermarkets.

Tofu: Silken usually comes in a carton and is not chilled, regular is chilled. Very different uses for them, so don't muddle them up!

Pastes: I tend to favour pastes for garlic, ginger, and chilli over fresh items as they keep longer and are much easier to use when you need them.

Seasonal: Buy what's grown locally and in season, or is hardy and shipped (e.g. bananas, not blueberries). This has a much lower impact on the environment.

Fresh vs. Frozen vs. Store Cupboard: Lowest impact is typically store cupboard, then frozen by a small margin, then fresh. If you can, try and buy items which are longer life.

Best Before Dates: If products in your kitchen are past their Best Before Date, they may still be okay to use. Check them and use reasonable judgement. Don't add to the statistics!

Weights, not volumes: All of the recipes in this book favour weights instead of volumes as this avoids making more equipment dirty. Less washing up for you.

MAINS

TOP TIP Soup is a great way to use old veg that is on the turn - e.g. try switching out the broccoli for cauliflower.

LEEK & POTATO SOUP

On a cold winter's day, nothing beats a hearty soup.

5 mins | 40 mins | 4 servings | Freezable | Vegan Friendly

INGREDIENTS

Knob of Veg/Baking Butter/Spread
2 Large/3 Medium Leeks (~400-500g)
4 Large Potatoes (~600-750g)
½ Head of Broccoli
1 tbsp Garlic Paste
1L Boiling Water
2 Vegetable Stock Cubes
1 tsp Salt
1 tsp Black Pepper
2 tsp Thyme
1 tbsp Nutritional Yeast (optional)

METHOD

1. Wash the leeks and potatoes (leave the skin on) and cut them roughly, making sure to cut around any bad bits in the potatoes. You can use the green part of the leek too, but cut off any wilted or limp parts. Also roughly chop the broccoli (you can use the stalk too).

2. In a large saucepan/pot, melt the butter on a medium-high heat. Add all of the veg and the garlic to the pot and cook for **10 minutes**, stirring regularly.

3. Crumble in the stock cubes and add enough boiling water to cover the top of the vegetables (roughly 800mL-1L). Reduce the heat, then put a lid on the pan and leave to cook for **20-30 minutes**, or until the potatoes have softened. Check and stir occasionally. Top up the water if the level drops below the top of the veg.

4. Stir in the salt, pepper, herbs, and nutritional yeast. Remove from the heat. Using a hand blender, puree the mix until smooth. (if you only have a stand blender, transfer to this and blend until smooth). If you prefer a thinner/runnier soup, add a little extra boiling water here.

Serve with a sprinkling of nutritional yeast, and herbs on top. Tastes great with a couple of pieces of toast.
Cover and store in the fridge for 2-3 days, or freeze in individual portions (make sure to defrost and reheat throroughly).

CARBON IMPACT CHECK

Per Serving	kg CO2 eq.	Compared
This Recipe	0.40	
Typical Recipe[1]	0.46	

NOTES:

....

....

....

SHORTCRUST PASTRY

Half fat to flour; just as good when plant based.

5 mins   15 mins   Freezable   *Vegan Friendly*

INGREDIENTS

Covered Pie (25cm):
320g Plain Flour
160g Veg/Baking Butter (Not Spread)
Large Pinch Salt
Water

Uncovered Pie (25cm):
As above, but 220g Flour, 110g Butter

Topped-Only Pie (25cm):
As above, but 100g Flour, 50g Butter

Covered Pie (20cm):
As above, but 240g Flour, 120g Butter

Uncovered Pie (20cm):
As above, but 160g Flour, 80g Butter

Topped-Only Pie (20cm):
As above, but 80g Flour, 40g Butter

TOP TIP Use a food processor on 'pulse' if you don't like getting your hands dirty!

METHOD

1. Rub the butter, flour, and salt together with your fingertips, until resembling breadcrumbs.
2. Add water, a splash at a time, and mix into the crumb mix. Continue until the mixture forms a dough. Try not to overwork the mixture.
3. Divide the dough as needed (e.g. base and lid). Roll out on a lightly floured work surface using a floured rolling pin. Lift and turn regularly to prevent it from sticking. Use your tin to work out how big to roll it.
4. Use the rolling pin to pick up the pastry and lay it in position. If making a base, slide the pastry down into any corners, making sure not to force and stretch it.
5. Trim off any excess, and use it to patch any holes (if you are making a base).

Blind Baking (if you are making a base):
6. Lay a baking liner/greaseproof paper loosely over the base and top with baking beans. You can use rice or dried beans if you don't have baking beans – just be sure not to lose any in the pastry.
7. Bake for **8-10 minutes** at **180°C (160°C Fan)** when required by the recipe. Carefully remove the baking beans and bake for a further **3-5 minutes**, until the base is golden.

You can chill (1-2 days) or freeze any spare in an airtight wrap or container. Alternatively, reroll it and add a dollop of jam before cooking for 10-15 minutes for some bonus treats.

CARBON IMPACT CHECK

Per 100g	kg CO2 eq.	Compared
This Recipe	0.19	
Typical Recipe[2]	0.37	

NOTES:

....

....

....

LEEK & MUSHROOM PIE

A pub classic gone plant-based.

15 mins   25 mins   4 servings   Freezable   **V** Vegan Friendly

INGREDIENTS

Shortcrust Pastry (see page 16)

Filling for 25cm Tin:
Knob of Veg/Baking Butter/Spread
1 Large Leek
1 Medium Onion
1 tbsp Garlic Paste
100-150g Mushrooms
120g Plant Cream
200g Plant Milk
1 Vegetable Stock Cube
100g Chicken-Style Pieces (optional)
2 tbsp Sage
1 tsp Salt
Plant Milk To Brush On Top

METHOD

1. You can choose if you want to have a base and a top, or just a top. If making a base, preheat the oven to **180°C (160°C Fan)**. Make the shortcrust pastry. If making a base, blind bake whilst preparing the filling. If not, then preheat the oven now.
2. Wash the leek and finely dice with the onion. Chop the mushrooms into quarters or smaller.
3. Melt the knob of butter in a large frying pan over a high heat. Add the leek and onion, and cook until slightly browned. Add the mushrooms and cook for a further **2-3 minutes**.
4. Crumble in the stock cube, and add the chicken-style pieces (optional), cream, milk, sage, salt, and garlic. Reduce the heat a little and cook until thickened.
5. Pour the filling into your pie-dish and top with your pastry. Brush the top with extra plant milk to give it a golden colour on baking.
6. Bake for **20-30 minutes**, until the top has turned golden.

TOP TIP: Use leftover pastry to decorate the top. Cut out shapes and stick them on with milk.

Serve with your choice of extra trimmings (e.g. new potatoes, more veg, etc.).
Transfer to an airtight container and store in the fridge for 2-3 days, or freeze (make sure to defrost and reheat throroughly).

CARBON IMPACT CHECK

Per Serving	kg CO2 eq.	Compared
This Recipe	0.51	
Typical Recipe[3]	2.03	

NOTES:

TOP TIP Choose your veg carefully. A lot of high water content veg may give you a soggy bottom!

QUICHE

The French classic you can make without breaking eggs.

20 mins   40 mins   4 servings   Freezable   Vegan Friendly

INGREDIENTS

Shortcrust Pastry (see page 16)

Filling for 25cm Tin:
Knob of Veg/Baking Butter/Spread
Choose 4x 150g of veg from:
- Mushrooms
- Leeks (approx. 1x medium)
- Onions (approx. 1x medium)
- Cherry tomatoes (you can use regular tomatoes but chop them up first)
- Fresh spinach (you can use frozen but make sure it has defrosted first)
- Broccoli (approx. half a head)
- Peas (frozen is fine, but defrost and drain them)

½ tsp Salt
1 tsp Black Pepper
1 pack of Silken Tofu (approx. 250-300g)
50g Plant Milk
6 tbsp Nutritional Yeast
1 tbsp Garlic Paste
½ tsp Paprika

Plant-Based Cheese To Top

Serve with your choice of extra trimmings (e.g. new potatoes, more veg, etc.).
Transfer to an airtight container and store in the fridge for 2-3 days, or freeze (make sure to defrost and reheat throroughly).

METHOD

1. Preheat the oven to **180°C (160°C Fan)**. Make the shortcrust pastry. Blind bake when instructed below.
2. Chop up all the veg as fine as you like it. Generally: quarter the mushrooms; dice the leeks; halve the cherry tomatoes; roughly chop the spinach; chop the broccoli into thumb sized pieces.
3. Heat the knob of butter in a large frying pan over a medium-high heat. Add your chosen veg in the following order, giving a few minutes between each addition: onions and leeks, broccoli, mushrooms, tomatoes, peas. Add half of the salt and pepper. Cook until the spinach has just wilted (lost its shape).
4. Blind bake the pastry as explained in the shortcrust recipe. Continue below whilst it cooks.
5. Put the remaining ingredients (except the cheese) into a blender and blend until smooth (you may need to scrape the edges down and re-blend).
6. Place half of the vegetables in the baked pastry, followed by the tofu mix, and then the other half of the vegetables on top. You can add some grated cheese cheese to the top for extra cheesy goodness.
7. Bake for **40-45 minutes** until the middle doesn't move when you wobble the dish.

CARBON IMPACT CHECK

Per Serving	kg CO2 eq.	Compared
This Recipe	0.54	
Typical Recipe[4]	1.19	

NOTES:

....

....

....

TOP
TIP
This recipe is really versatile. Try other vegetable combinations and keep a note of your favourites.

SAVOURY CRUMBLE

The closest thing to an all-in-one Sunday Roast.

20 mins   25 mins   6 servings   Freezable   Vegan Friendly

INGREDIENTS

Topping:
75g Plain Flour
75g Oats
100g Stuffing Mix
100g Vegetable/Baking Butter/Spread
½ tsp Salt
½ tsp Black Pepper

Filling:
Knob of Vegetable/Baking Butter/Spread
1 Large Onion
1 Large Carrot
2-3 Large Potatoes (~500g)
100g Mushrooms
75g Peas
100g Chicken-Style Pieces/Other Meat Alternative
1 tbsp Onion Gravy Granules
250-300mL Boiling Water
½ tsp Salt
1 tsp Sage

Nutritional Yeast

METHOD

1. In a medium bowl, mix all of the topping ingredients together until resembling breadcrumbs. Set aside for later.
2. Wash the carrot and potatoes (leave the skins on if you want) and cut them into cubes of approximately 0.5cm in size, removing any blemishes as you go. Dice the onion.
3. Preheat the oven to **180°C (160°C Fan)**.
4. In a large frying pan, melt the butter on a medium-high heat. Add the potatoes, carrot and onion to the pot and cook for **10 minutes**, stirring regularly.
5. Meanwhile, roughly cut the mushrooms into quarters. Add them to the pan with the peas, chicken-style pieces, gravy granules, water, salt, and sage. Cook for a further **5 minutes**, stirring regularly. Add more water as necessary to keep the sauce at a consistency you like.
6. Pour the filling mix into a large ovenproof dish and spread it to the edges. Sprinkle the crumble mix evenly over the top. Finish with a topping of nutrional yeast.
7. Bake for **20-30 minutes**, until the top has turned golden.

Serve with your choice of extra trimmings (e.g. Yorkshire puddings, more veg, etc.) and more gravy as you like it. Transfer to an airtight container and store in the fridge for 2-3 days, or freeze (make sure to defrost and reheat throroughly).

CARBON IMPACT CHECK

Per Serving	kg CO2 eq.	Compared
This Recipe	0.37	
Typical Recipe[5]	3.27	

NOTES:

COTTAGE PIE

A home comfort made healthier and lower carbon.

10 mins · 50 mins · 6 servings · Freezable · **V** Vegan Friendly

INGREDIENTS

Mash:
1.2kg Potatoes
150-175g Plant Milk (depending on how thick you like your mash)
30g Butter/Spread
Salt and Black Pepper To Your Taste

Base:
Knob of Veg Butter/Spread/Splash of Oil
1 Medium Onion (red or white)
1 Large Carrot
½ Aubergine (fry up the rest with some salt and pepper on toast for breakfast)
100g Mushrooms
1 Can of Chopped Tomatoes
1 Can of Green Lentils (drained)
400g Meat-Free Mince
1 Vegetable Stock Cube
450mL Boiling Water
2 tbsp Onion Gravy Granules
1 tbsp Soy Sauce
1 tbsp Mixed Herbs
1 tsp Salt
½ tsp Black Pepper

Plant Based Cheese and/or Nutritional Yeast to top.

Cover and store in the fridge for 2-3 days, or freeze in individual portions (make sure to defrost and reheat throroughly).

METHOD

1. Half fill a medium-large saucepan with boiling water and place on a medium heat. Wash the potatoes and chop out any blemishes. Peel (optional) and chop into thumb sized cubes. Add to the pan, topping up the water if needed. Check the potatoes occasionally using a knife (see #6).
2. Whilst the potatoes cook, dice the onion and carrot and fry in a large pan on a medium heat with the oil/butter/spread until softened.
3. Cut the aubergine into small cubes and quarter the mushrooms. Add them to the pan with the mince, lentils and chopped tomatoes.
4. Crumble the stock cube into the pan and add 450mL boiling water, the gravy granules, soy sauce, herbs, salt, and pepper.
5. Reduce to a low heat and leave to simmer and thicken, stirring occasionally. Add extra water if needed.
6. When the potatoes slide off of an inserted knife, they are ready to mash. Drain the pan and add the remaining mash ingredients. Mash with a fork or masher until smooth.
7. Assemble the pie in an over-proof dish/dishes, placing a layer of mince mixture, followed by a layer of mash.
8. Add some grated plant cheese and/or nutritional yeast and place under a grill for **5-10 minutes** until crispy.

CARBON IMPACT CHECK

Per Serving	kg CO2 eq.	Compared
This Recipe	0.72	
Typical Recipe[6]	3.82	

NOTES:

....

....

....

JOLLOF RICE

An East African dish that deserves more attention.

5 mins   30 mins   6 servings   Freezable   Vegan Friendly

INGREDIENTS

2 Medium Onions
2 Tins of Chopped Tomatoes
250g Passata
2-3 tbsp Chilli Paste (depending on how hot you want)
2 tsp Medium Curry Powder
2 tbsp Garlic Paste
1 tsp Ground Ginger
2 Vegetable Stock Cubes

200g Frozen Mixed Veg
100g Frozen Peas (or more mixed veg)
100g Chicken-Style Pieces
400g Basmati or Long-Grain Rice
750mL-1L Boiling Water

METHOD

1. Roughly chop the onions. Put them into a blender with the tomatoes, passata, chilli paste, garlic paste, ground ginger, and stock cubes. Blend until mostly smooth. If your blender isn't big enough, do this in 2 batches and combine at step 2.
2. Pour the mix into a large pan over a medium-high heat. Cook and stir until the colour becomes a brick red and the stock cubes have dissolved (approx. **10 minutes**).
3. Add the mixed veg, peas, chicken-style pieces, and rice. Stir until well combined.
4. Add about half of the water and stir. Reduce the heat, cover, and simmer for about **20 minutes**. Stir the mixture regularly, and top-up the water as it starts to absorb into the rice. Add about half of the boiling water and stir to combine. Continue until the rice is cooked (soft).

Great served on its own, like a risotto, or with fried plantain.
Rice can be stored and reheated, but should be stored in the fridge as soon as possible after cooking and thoroughly reheated. Transfer to an airtight container and store in the fridge for 1-2 days, or freeze (make sure to defrost and reheat throroughly).

CARBON IMPACT CHECK

Per Serving	kg CO2 eq.	Compared
This Recipe	0.94	
Typical Recipe[7]	0.97	

NOTES:

....

....

....

....

TOP
TIP

Keep hold of the chickpea water, called 'Aquafaba'.
You can make all sorts with it (see page 67).

CHILLI NON-CARNE

How hot can you handle?

10 mins   35 mins   4 servings   Freezable   Vegan Friendly

INGREDIENTS

1 Red Onion
Splash Vegetable Oil
1 Pepper
200g Plant-Based Mince
1 can Chickpeas
1 can Red Kidney Beans
1 can Chopped Tomatoes
250g Passata
2-3 tbsp Chilli Paste (or more if you want)
1 tbsp Smoked Paprika
2 tsp Ground Coriander
1 tsp Salt
1 tsp Pepper
1 tbsp Lemon Juice/Lime Juice

METHOD

1. Dice the onions and put them in a large pan over a medium-high heat with the oil until softened.
2. Slice the pepper into strips and add to the pan. Cook until slightly browned.
3. Drain the chickpeas and beans, then add with the remaining ingredients to the pan and stir well. Reduce the heat, cover with a lid and allow to simmer for around **15-20 minutes** until thickened.

Serve with your choice of rice, bulgar wheat, couscous, or other grain.
Transfer to an airtight container and store in the fridge for 2-3 days, or freeze (make sure to defrost and reheat throroughly).

CARBON IMPACT CHECK

Per Serving	kg CO2 eq.	Compared
This Recipe	0.87	
Typical Recipe[8]	3.14	

NOTES:

TOP TIP Try other stir fry veg if you like. Just be careful not to buy things which are out of season.

NUTTY STIR-FRY

Asia on your doorstep with less carbon.

10 mins   15 mins   4 servings   Freezable   Vegan Friendly

INGREDIENTS

3 tbsp Garlic Paste
1 tbsp Ground Ginger
1 Onion
Splash Sesame/Vegetable Oil
Choose 4x 100g of veg from:
- Mushrooms
- Baby Corns
- Sugar Snap Peas
- Broccoli
- Pepper
- Carrot

100g Peanut Butter
80g Soy Sauce
50g Golden Syrup
2 tbsp Chilli Paste (or more if you want)
150-200mL Water
½ tsp Salt

METHOD

1. Dice the onions and put them in a large pan over a medium-high heat with the oil, garlic, and ginger, until softened.
2. Prepare the remaining veg as follows: slice the mushrooms; third the corns; chop the broccoli into thumb sized pieces; slice the pepper into strips; cut the carrot into matchsticks. Add to the pan and stir regularly until slightly softened.
3. Add the remaining ingredients to the pan and stir well. Continue to cook for another **5-10 minutes**, until the sauce is well combined, veg is coated, and the hardest vegetables you have used have softened.

Serve with your choice of noodles and an extra splash of soy sauce.
Transfer to an airtight container and store in the fridge for 2-3 days.
You can also freeze the stir fry, but be sure to mix well when defrosting as it may slightly separate (make sure to defrost and reheat throroughly). Cooked noodles don't keep so well so are best eaten in the first sitting.

CARBON IMPACT CHECK

Per Serving	kg CO2 eq.	Compared
This Recipe	0.33	
Typical Recipe[9]	0.76	

NOTES:

....

....

....

TOP TIP Noodles often contain egg. Udon and rice noodles are safe bets, but keep an eye out.

NOODLE SOUP

You can do better than instant noodles.

15 mins   20 mins   4 servings   Not Freezable   Vegan Friendly

INGREDIENTS

1 pack of Regular Tofu (250-300g, drained)
3-5 tbsp Cournflour
4-6 tbsp Vegetable Oil

75-100g Pak-Choi or Green Cabbage
1 Carrot
1 can of Water Chestnuts (225g/140g drained)
100g Beansprouts (you can buy these canned to last longer)
100g Sping Onions (~1 bundle)
150g Mushrooms
2 tbsp Garlic Paste
1 tbsp Ginger Paste
1½ tbsp Miso Paste
1 tbsp Tahini
2 Vegetable Stock Cubes
1L Boiling Water
3 tbsp Soy Sauce
200-300g Noodles (approx. 75g per person)

METHOD

1. Cut the tofu into cubes of roughly 1-2cm in size. Dice the spring onions; slice the mushrooms; peel and cut the carrot into thin batons; and cut the pak-choi/cabbage into thick strips. Drain the water chestnuts.
2. Add the vegetables (except the pak-choi/cabbage), pastes, tahini, stock cubes, water, and soy sauce to a large sauce pan. Place the pan over a medium heat, and simmer for **8-10 minutes**, until the carrot has softened a little.
3. Meanwhile, roll each cube of tofu in the cornflour to cost.
4. Heat the oil in a small pan on a high heat. When the pan is hot, add the tofu pieces and cook until crispy on each side. Be careful as you turn them to prevent breaking the coating off or crumbling the tofu. Set to one side.
5. Add the pak-choi/cabbage and noodles to the vegetable pan and heat for a further **2-3 minutes**.
6. Serve the vegetable-noodle broth in bowls, with the crispy tofu pieces on top.

Serve with further beansprouts and pak-choi/cabbage for a little crunch.
Transfer to an airtight container and store in the fridge for 1-2 days. Sadly this recipe is not freezable.
The pastes used in this recipe can last a long time in the fridge. You can also freeze tahini, ginger paste, and garlic paste if you need to.

CARBON IMPACT CHECK

Per Serving	kg CO2 eq.	Compared
This Recipe	0.48	
Typical Recipe[10]	0.90	

NOTES:

....

....

....

TOP TIP Watch out for anchovies in the curry paste. It's an annoying ingredient that can catch you out.

THAI GREEN CURRY

A good excuse for eating sticky rice too.

 10 mins   20 mins   6 servings   Not Freezable V Vegan Friendly

INGREDIENTS

Splash of Vegetable Oil
Choose 5 of:
- 100g Spring Onions (~1 bundle)
- 1 Carrot
- ½ Head of Broccoli
- 1 can of Water Chestnuts (225g/140g drained)
- 1 can of Bamboo Shoots (225g/120g drained)
- 1 Pepper
- ½ Aubergine
- 75g Sugar Snap Peas
- 75g Baby Corn
- 75g Green Beans

1 pack of Regular Tofu (250-300g, drained)
1 tbsp Garlic Paste
1 tbsp Ginger Paste
3-4 tbsp Thai Green Curry Paste
2 cans of Coconut Milk
1-2 tsp Chilli Paste
2 tsp Mixed Herbs
½ tsp Salt
½ tsp Black Pepper
1 tbsp Brown Sugar

METHOD

1. Prepare the vegetables. Chop the carrot into matchsticks; chop the broccoli into small florets; drain the water chestnuts and bamboo shoots; slice the pepper into small strips; cube the aubergine; remove the ends and halve the peas, beans, and corn. Also cut the tofu into cubes of about 1.5cm in size.
2. In a large pan over a high heat, cook the oil and onions with the garlic, ginger, and curry pastes, until the onions soften a little.
3. Add the carrot and broccoli. Cook for a further 3-5 minutes, until softened a little.
4. Reduce the heat a little, then add the tofu, chestnuts, bamboo shoots, pepper, peas, corn, beans, coconut milk, herbs, salt, pepper, and sugar. Simmer for **3-5 minutes**, until all the vegetables have cooked and sauce has thickened.

Serve with your choice of rice; sticky thai rice is a favourite. Garnish with extra pak-choi (or similar).
Transfer to an airtight container and store in the fridge for 2-3 days. This recipe does not freeze so well as you lose the structure of the vegetables on defrosting.

CARBON IMPACT CHECK

Per Serving	kg CO2 eq.	Compared
This Recipe	0.45	
Typical Recipe[11]	0.64	

NOTES:

TOP TIP Other nuts can work really well in curries too. Try some almonds next time instead.

DHINGRI MATAR CURRY

Inspired by my local curry house, now yours to enjoy.

5 mins   20 mins   6 servings   Freezable   Vegan Friendly

INGREDIENTS

400g Mushrooms (preferably button)
130g Frozen Peas
200g Chicken-Style Pieces
½ Aubergine
400g Passata
1½ tsp Garam Masala
½ tsp Turmeric
1-2 tbsp Chilli Paste
1½ tbsp Ginger Paste/2 tbsp Ground Ginger
100g Cashews
½ tsp Ground Coriander
150mL Water
1 tsp Salt

METHOD

1. Cut the aubergine into 1cm cubes and halve or quarter the mushrooms. Add them both to a large saucepan over a medium-high heat.
2. Add the chicken-style pieces and cook for about 5 minutes.
3. Add the remaining ingredients and stir to combine.
4. Reduce the heat slightly and allow to simmer for a further **8-12 minutes**, until thickened a little and cooked through.

Serve with your choice of rice and/or naan. Use a toaster to cook your naan quickly and efficiently.
Transfer to an airtight container and store in the fridge for 2-3 days, or freeze (make sure to defrost and reheat throroughly).

CARBON IMPACT CHECK

Per Serving	kg CO2 eq.	Compared
This Recipe	0.70	
Typical Recipe[12]	0.99	

NOTES:

....

....

....

TOP TIP Try eating this the traditional way with no knife and fork. Grab a naan and off you go!

LENTIL DAHL

An accompaniment or worthy dish in its own right.

10 mins   40 mins   4 servings   Freezable   **V** Vegan Friendly

INGREDIENTS

Splash of Vegetable Oil
1 Onion
2 tbsp Garlic Paste
400g Butternut Squash (~½ of a squash)
1 can of Chopped Tomatoes
1 can of Coconut Milk
300g Red Lentils
600mL Boiling Water
1 Vegetable Stock Cube
½ tsp Cayenne Pepper
1 tsp Ground Coriander
1 tsp Ground Turmeric
2 tsp Ground Cumin

METHOD

1. Peel and cut the butternut squash into 1-2cm cubes. Dice the onion.
2. Transfer the onion to a large pan over a medium-high heat with the oil until softened.
3. Crumble in the stock cube, then add the squash, cayenne pepper, cumin, coriander, turmeric, garlic, tomatoes, coconut milk, and water. Stir until combined and bubbling.
4. Reduce the heat and simmer for **10 minutes.** Add the lentils and continue to simmer for a further **15-20 minutes**, until the lentils have softened. Add more water if needed.

Serve with a sprinkling of fresh coriander and your choice of rice and/or naan. Alternatively, serve as a side to a curry banquet.
Transfer to an airtight container and store in the fridge for 2-3 days, or freeze (make sure to defrost and reheat throroughly).

CARBON IMPACT CHECK

This dish is traditionally plant-based anyway, meaning there is very little to compare. It is already a low emission dish, and hopefully you enjoy this take on it.

NOTES:

....

....

....

TOP TIP Great with a glass of white wine, but also try throwing a glass into the mix as well.

RISOTTO

Another hard to resist one-pot staple.

10 mins   30 mins   6 servings   Freezable   V Vegan Friendly

INGREDIENTS

Knob of Vegetable/Baking Butter/Spread
2 Small White Onions
200g Mushrooms (button are best to avoid a grey risotto)
½ Butternut Squash
1 Vegetable Stock Cube
130g Frozen Peas
10 tbsp Nutritional Yeast
1 tsp Salt
½ tsp Black Pepper
2 tbsp Garlic Paste
1 tbsp Mixed Herbs
250-300g Risotto Rice
1.2-1.5L Boiling Water
50-100g Plant Cream (optional)

METHOD

1. Dice the onions and put them in a large pan over a medium-high heat with the oil until softened.
2. Halve the mushrooms and peel and cube the butternut squash. Add them to the pan and cook until the squash has softened a little.
3. Crumble in the stock cube, and add the nutritional yeast, garlic paste, salt, pepper, and herbs.
4. Scatter the rice on top and add about 1L of the water. Bring to the boil and then reduce the heat to a simmer. Continue to stir for **8-10 minutes**, until the rice has expanded and is slightly softened. Add more water as the level reduces.
5. Add the peas and cream (optional) and mix in. Continue to simmer for **5-10 minutes**, until the rice is soft.

Serve with a sprinkling of nutritional yeast and herbs.
Rice can be stored and reheated, but should be stored in the fridge as soon as possible after cooking and thoroughly reheated. Transfer to an airtight container and store in the fridge for 2-3 days, or freeze (make sure to defrost and reheat throroughly).

CARBON IMPACT CHECK

Per Serving	kg CO2 eq.	Compared
This Recipe	0.68	
Typical Recipe[13]	0.95	

NOTES:

....

....

....

TOP TIP — If you want a more traditionally coloured carbonara, drop the mushrooms and add a little turmeric.

PASTA CARBONARA

Not an egg in sight with this re-imagined Italian classic.

10 mins   20 mins   4 servings   Freezable   *Vegan Friendly*

INGREDIENTS

Splash of Vegetable Oil
1 White Onion
150g Plant-Based Bacon or Smoked Tofu
100-150g Mushrooms (button are best to avoid a grey sauce)
1 pack of Silken Tofu (250-300g, don't drain)
3 tbsp Garlic Paste
2 tbsp Soy Sauce
6 tbsp Nutritional Yeast
2 tbsp Lemon Juice
1 tsp Salt
½ tsp Smoked Paprika
½ tsp Black Pepper
2 tbsp Mixed Herbs
50g Plant Milk
50g Plant Cream (optional)

350g Pasta (choose what shape you like)

METHOD

1. In a medium pan, set the pasta to boil on a medium heat. Use a lid as this will save you energy.
2. In a blender, combine the milk, cream (optional), silken tofu, garlic paste, soy sauce, lemon juice, nutritional yeast, salt, pepper, paprika, and herbs. Blend until smooth. Set to one side.
3. Dice the onion, bacon/smoked tofu, and mushrooms, and cook them with the oil in a large pan over a medium-high heat until the onion has softened and the bacon/tofu has started to crisp.
4. Reduce the heat and add the sauce from the blender. Stir until well combined.
5. When cooked, drain the pasta but keep a little of the water. Add the pasta to the pan and stir until well coated. If it is a little thick, you can use the pasta water you kept to thin it down.

Serve with a sprinkling of herbs and garlic some bread. Transfer to an airtight container and store in the fridge for 2-3 days, or freeze (make sure to defrost and reheat throroughly).

CARBON IMPACT CHECK

Per Serving	kg CO2 eq.	Compared
This Recipe	0.43	
Typical Recipe[14]	0.76	

NOTES:

....

....

....

TOP TIP Wholewheat pasta can boost the fibre in this dish and make you feel fuller for longer.

TOMATO & MEATBALL PASTA

Who doesn't love it!?

5 mins | 20 mins | 4 servings | Freezable | Vegan Friendly

INGREDIENTS

Splash of Vegetable Oil
1 Red Onion
2 tbsp Garlic Paste
1 Pepper
250-350g Plant-Based Meatballs (approx. 12)
100-150g Mushrooms
1 can of Chopped Tomatoes
3 tbsp Tomato Puree
250g Passata
1 tsp Salt
½ tsp Black Pepper
1 tbsp Oregano
1 tbsp Basil

METHOD

1. Dice the onion and cook it with the garlic in a large pan over a medium-high heat with the oil until softened.
2. Slice the pepper into small pieces and quarter the mushrooms. Add them to the pan with the meatballs. Cook until the meatballs have slightly browned.
3. Add the remaining ingredients and reduce the heat a little. Stir well to combine. Cook until the sauce has thickened to your desired consistency (typically around **8-10 minutes**). Now would be a good time to put your pasta on to cook.

Serve with your choice of pasta. Top with a little plant-based cheese.
If you swap the meatballs for plant-based mince, this makes a great bolognese.
Transfer to an airtight container and store in the fridge for 2-3 days, or freeze (make sure to defrost and reheat throroughly).

CARBON IMPACT CHECK

Per Serving	kg CO2 eq.	Compared
This Recipe	0.97	
Typical Recipe[15]	3.17	

NOTES:

....

....

....

TOP TIP Like an extra crispy top? Put the lasagne under the grill for 10 minutes at the end of cooking.

LASAGNE

Just as cheesy but much lower impact and a lot less effort.

35 mins | 30 mins | 6 servings | Freezable | Vegan Friendly

INGREDIENTS

Splash of Vegetable Oil
1 Onion
1 tbsp Garlic Paste
150-200g Mushrooms
1 Courgette
1 Pepper
1 can of Chopped Tomatoes
250g Pasatta
150g Dried Red Lentils
100g Spinach (frozen is fine, defrost first)
1 tbsp Mixed Herbs
2 tbsp Soy Sauce
½ tsp Salt
½ tsp Black Pepper
½ tsp Paprika (not smoked)
700mL Boiling Water
170g Plant-Based Cream Cheese (garlic and herb is preferable)
10-12 Dried Lasagne Sheets

Plant-Based Cheese and Nutritional Yeast to Top

Serve on its own or with your choice of additonal vegetables.
Transfer to an airtight container and store in the fridge for 2-3 days, or freeze (make sure to defrost and reheat throroughly).

METHOD

1. Pre-heat the oven to **200°C (180°C Fan)**.
2. Prepare the vegtables by dicing the onions; slicing the courgette into half-discs; and the pepper into small chunks.
3. In a large pan over a medium-high heat, cook the onion and garlic in the oil until the onion has softened.
4. Add the mushrooms, courgette and pepper. Continue to cook for about **10 minutes**, until the pepper and courgette have softened.
5. Add the spinach, lentils, tomatoes, and passata, herbs, soy sauce, salt, pepper, and paprika, and stir until well combined. Reduce the heat to a simmer and cook for about **15 minutes**, adding the boiling wter gradually. Cook until the lentils have softened.
6. Meanwhile spread the cream cheese on one side of all of the lasagne sheets. This is a trick to save you making an extra sauce.
7. Pour about a third of the filling mix into a large ovenproof dish, then top with lasagne sheets (cheese side down). Repeat for a second layer. Top with the final third of filling and sprinkle with plant-based cheese and nutritional yeast.
8. Bake for **30-40 minutes**, until the pasta has softened, and vegetable mix is bubbling.

CARBON IMPACT CHECK

Per Serving	kg CO2 eq.	Compared
This Recipe	1.01	
Typical Recipe[16]	1.70	

NOTES:

....

....

....

TOP TIP: Would you like fries with that? Make your own with sliced potatoes, a little oil, and 20 mins in the oven.

BEAN BURGERS

No disintegrating patties here.

20 mins   30 mins   4 servings   Freezable   Vegan Friendly

INGREDIENTS

1 can of Dark Beans (e.g. Pinto/Red Kidney/Borlotti/Black)
1 Large Sweet Potato (~400g)
1 Onion
100g Long Grain/Basmati Rice
2½ tsp Cumin
1½ tsp Smoked Paprika
1 tsp Black Pepper
1 tbsp Mixed Herbs
1 tbsp Tomato Puree
1 tsp Salt
1 tbsp Garlic Paste

METHOD

1. Pre-heat the oven to **190°C (170°C Fan)**. Lightly grease or line a large baking tray.
2. In a small pan, boil the rice on a low heat until soft. Line or grease a large baking tray.
3. Meanwhile, roughly chop the sweet potato and put it in a microwaveable bowl with a little water. Microwave on high for **3-5 minutes**, until very soft. Drain ainy remaining water.
4. Finely dice the onion and place in a large bowl with the remaining ingredients, except the beans.
5. Add the sweet potato and mash until no potato chunks remain.
6. Drain the beans and add half of the tin to the mix. Drain the rice and also add to the mix. Mash until fairly smooth. Stir in the remaining beans.
7. Form the mix into 8-10 patties and place onto the baking tray.
8. Bake for **30-40 minutes**, until crispy on the outside.

Serve in a bread roll with your choice of salad fillings and sauce. If you have more sweet potatoes, you could chop them up and oven bake them for fries.
These burgers can be stored and reheated, but should be stored in the fridge as soon as possible after cooking and thoroughly reheated. Transfer to an airtight container and store in the fridge for 1-2 days, or freeze (make sure to defrost and reheat throroughly).

CARBON IMPACT CHECK

Per Serving	kg CO2 eq.	Compared
This Recipe	0.32	
Typical Recipe[17]	2.98	

NOTES:

....

....

....

TOP TIP Trimmings with a roast can be made lower impact by using plant-based spreads instead of animal fats.

LENTIL "MEAT" LOAF

An excellent alternative at Christmas or a Sunday roast.

20 mins   40 mins   6+ servings   Freezable   Vegan Friendly

INGREDIENTS

Splash of Vegetable Oil
1 Onion
3 tbsp Garlic Paste
1 Carrot
1 Parsnip
150g Mushrooms Plain Flour
1 can of Dark Beans (e.g. Pinto/Red Kidney/Borlotti/Black)
1 can of Green Lentils
120g Rolled Oats
3 tbsp Soy Sauce
3 tbsp Mixed Herbs
6 tbsp Nutritional Yeast
½ tsp Salt
½ tsp Black Pepper

METHOD

1. Preheat the oven to **180°C (160°C Fan)**. Lightly grease or line a 20cm loaf tin.
2. Prepare the vegetables: dice the onion; grate the carrot and the parsnip; and quarter the mushrooms.
3. In a large saucepan over a medium-high heat, add the onion, carrot, parsnip, and oil. Cook until softened.
4. Drain the beans and lentils and add to the pan with the mushrooms. Cook until the mushrooms are slightly softened.
5. Remove from the heat and add the remaining ingredients. Use a masher to combine the ingredients until they come together. You do not want to mash unil smooth as this will remove the texture.
6. Transfer the mixture to the loaf tin and smooth the top so it is level. Bake for **35-45 minutes**, until the top has crispedan is slightly browned.

Serve with your choice of extra trimmings (e.g. Yorkshire puddings, more veg, etc.) and gravy as you like it.
Transfer to an airtight container and store in the fridge for 2-3 days, or freeze (make sure to defrost and reheat throroughly).

CARBON IMPACT CHECK

Per Serving	kg CO2 eq.	Compared
This Recipe	0.28	
Typical Recipe[18]	3.05	

NOTES:

....

....

....

DESSERTS

TOP TIP   This is an easy one to make gluten-free. Just swap out the flour and oats for gluten-free alternatives.

FRUIT CRUMBLE

A school dinner classic, just lower carbon.

10 mins   25 mins   6 servings   Freezable   V *Vegan Friendly*

INGREDIENTS

150g Plain Flour
125g White Sugar
100g Vegetable/Baking Butter/Spread
100g Rolled Oats
500g Fruit (frozen is fine, but defrost first)

METHOD

1. Pre-heat the oven to **180°C (160°C Fan)**. Dig out a large oven-proof dish or several small dishes.
2. Prepare the fruit as needed (e.g. chop apples, etc.), then spread the fruit in the dish, and scatter 50g of the sugar on top.
3. Weigh all of the remaining ingredients into a single bowl. Rub the ingredients together until they resemble breadcrumbs. You will find a food processor will make this a lot faster.
4. Scatter the crumble evenly on top of the fruit and bake in the oven for **25-35 minutes**, until the top is slightly browned and the fruit is bubbling.

Best served with a healthy portion of custard. Did you know most custard powders are dairy free?
Cover and store on the side for 2-3 days. Any leftovers will also freeze well.

CARBON IMPACT CHECK

Per Serving	kg CO2 eq.	Compared
This Recipe	0.26	
Typical Recipe[19]	0.29	

NOTES:

....

....

....

TOP TIP Try making the pie as little tartlets. Use a fairy cake tin and minaturise everything... great for parties.

FRUIT PIE

Looks impressive, but so simple to do.

20 mins   40 mins   6 servings   Freezable   **V** Vegan Friendly

INGREDIENTS

Shortcrust Pastry, but sweetened (see page 16: 25cm base <u>and</u> top, but add 80g sugar, 1 tbsp oil, and 1 tbsp water)

600g Fruit (frozen is fine, but defrost first)
50g Sugar

15g Plant Milk
1 tsp Golden Syrup/Maple Syrup/Agave Nectar

METHOD

1. Make and blind bake the sweetened shortcrust pastry on page 16. Leave to cool.
2. Prepare the fruit as needed (e.g. chop apples, etc.), then spread the fruit in the pastry case, and scatter the sugar on top.
3. Use the remaining pastry to create a top for the pie. If you are feeling up for a challenge, create a lattice by weaving strips of pastry (see picture).
4. Mix the milk and syrup together and brush on the top of the pastry. Bake in the oven for **20-30 minutes**, until the fruit is bubbling and the the top is slightly browned.

Decorate with a dusting of icing sugar and fresh fruit. Transfer to an airtight container and store on the side for 2-3 days. The complete pie, or any leftovers can also be frozen.

CARBON IMPACT CHECK

Per Serving	kg CO2 eq.	Compared
This Recipe	0.35	
Typical Recipe[20]	0.48	

NOTES:

....

....

....

TOP TIP Using dark brown sugar in this recipe gives it a much more toffee-like taste – the darker the better.

STICKY TOFFEE PUDDING

Everyone's favourite, made in just one pot.

10 mins   20 mins   6 servings   Freezable   *Vegan Friendly*

INGREDIENTS

Pudding:
250g Chopped Dates (dates can be tough to chop - saves a lot of time)
100g Vegetable/Baking Butter/Spread
200g Plant Milk
60g Dark Brown Sugar
200g Plain Flour
1½ tsp Bicarbonate of Soda

Sauce:
75g Plant Butter/Spread
100g Dark Brown Sugar
200g Plant Based Cream
½ tsp Salt

METHOD

1. Pre-heat the oven to **180°C (160°C Fan)**. Lightly grease or line a 23cm/9-inch square baking tin.
2. In a medium saucepan, add the milk, butter, and chopped dates. Gently heat until the butter has melted; liquid has thickened; and dates softened.
3. Remove from the heat and add the remaining cake ingredients. Mix until smooth except for the small date pieces.
4. Pour and spread into the tin and bake in the oven for **20-25 minutes**, until an inserted knife/skewer comes out clean. Cool on a rack.
5. For the sauce, add all of the ingredients into the pan used for the cake. Heat gently until the butter has melted and the sauce is smooth. Pour half of the sauce over the cake whilst it is still warm. Use the rest when serving.

Serve pieces of the cake with a generous splash of sauce. Also great with some extra custard or ice cream, for an extravagant pudding experience.
Store the cake in an airtight container for 3-4 days. or can be frozen. The sauce is best made fresh, but can be stored in an airtight container in the fridge for 1-2 days.

CARBON IMPACT CHECK

Per Serving	kg CO2 eq.	Compared
This Recipe	0.31	
Typical Recipe[21]	0.82	

NOTES:

....

....

....

MOLTEN CHOCOLATE PUD

Something great from so little. A favourite in my family.

5 mins   40 mins   6 servings   Freezable   Vegan Friendly

INGREDIENTS

Step 2:
50g Drinking Chocolate Powder
175g Plain Flour
1½ tsp Baking Powder
Large Pinch of Salt
50g White Sugar
120g Plant Milk
20g Vegetable Oil

Step 3:
50g Drinking Chocolate Powder
50g White Sugar

Step 4:
350mL Boiling Water

METHOD

1. Pre-heat the oven to **180°C (160°C Fan)**.
2. Weigh the step 2 ingredients into an oven proof dish and mix until a smooth paste has formed.
3. Sprinkle the step 3 ingredients on top of the paste.
4. Pour the boiling water on top but DO NOT STIR.
5. Transfer to the oven and cook for **40 minutes**.

Serve whilst warm with some plant-based cream or ice-cream.
Cover and eat within 2 days of making. Add a splash of water when reheating to refresh the sauce. You can freeze the pudding too, but transfer to an airtight container first.

CARBON IMPACT CHECK

Per Serving	kg CO2 eq.	Compared
This Recipe	0.09	
Typical Recipe[22]	0.86	

NOTES:

....

....

....

TOP TIP
If you haven't got any ramekins, use a deep muffin tin with cake cases. Some mugs may also work.

FRUITY PUDDING POTS

Known by another name in my house, but a favourite nonetheless.

10 mins   30 mins   4 servings   Freezable   Vegan Friendly

INGREDIENTS

150g Berries (frozen are fine, but make sure you've defrosted them)
50g Vegetable/Baking Butter/Spread
150ml Plant Milk
50g Sugar
100g Plain Flour
1½ tsp Baking Powder

METHOD

1. Pre-heat the oven to **190°C (170°C Fan)**.
2. Fill the bottom of 4-5 ramekins with the fruit.
3. Mix the flour, sugar and butter together until it resembles breadcrumbs. Add the milk and stir until a slightly lumpy batter forms.
4. Pour the batter over the fruit, keeping it even between the ramekins.
5. Bake in the oven for **30-40 minutes**, until the tops are risen and slightly golden.

Serve on a saucer whilst warm (be careful!). They will sink after a few minutes, so they are best served straight from the oven. Goes well with a little plant-based cream on top.
Best served fresh from the oven, but can be reheated. They could also be frozen if needed. Freeze in individual portions.

CARBON IMPACT CHECK

Per Serving	kg CO2 eq.	Compared
This Recipe	0.16	
Typical Recipe[23]	0.32	

NOTES:

CRUMBLE CAKE

What do you get if you cross a cake and a pudding?

15 mins   30 mins   8 servings   Freezable   Vegan Friendly

INGREDIENTS

500g Fruit (whatever you fancy, frozen is fine)
3 tbsp White Sugar

125g Vegetable/Baking Butter/Spread
100g White Sugar
1½ tbsp Vegetable Oil
1½ tbsp Water
2 tsp Baking Powder
25g Corn Flour
225g Plain Flour

METHOD

1. Pre-heat the oven to **200°C (180°C Fan)**. Lightly grease or line a 20cm cake tin.
2. In a small saucepan over a medium heat, gently warm the fruit and 3 tbsp sugar until softened. The juices will form a slight sauce. Put to one side to cool.
3. In a mixing bowl, combine the remaining ingredients and stir until combined.
4. Spoon two-thirds of the batter into your tin and spread evenly. Pour the fruit on top of this layer and spread evenly. Top the fruit with scoops of the remaining batter.
5. Cook for **30-35 minutes**, until the top has just started to brown.

Best served with plant-based cream, or custard.
Transfer to an airtight container and store on the side for 2-3 days. You can also freeze the finished cake.

CARBON IMPACT CHECK

Per Serving	kg CO2 eq.	Compared
This Recipe	0.21	
Typical Recipe[24]	0.37	

NOTES:

....

....

....

Test the filling on a cold plate to see if it will set. If not, then keep heating gently.

BUTTERSCOTCH TART

Another school dinner classic, now in your home.

30 mins   2-3 hours   8 servings   Freezable   *Vegan Friendly*

INGREDIENTS

Shortcrust Pastry, but sweetened (see page 16: 25cm base only, but add 80g sugar, 1 tbsp oil, and 1 tbsp water)

210g Vegetable/Baking Butter (Not Spread)
235g Demerara Sugar
130g Plant Milk
75g Plain Flour

METHOD

1. Make and blind bake the sweetened shortcrust pastry for **15-20 minutes**. Leave to cool.
2. In a medium saucepan, melt the butter and sugar together over a medium heat.
3. Reduce the heat. Add the plant milk and stir to combine.
4. Slowly add the flour in small quantities, mixing fast to avoid lumps. An electric mixer or whisk may help here.
5. Return to a medium heat and continue to stir until butterscotch starts to coat the back of the spoon.
6. Remove from the heat and pour into the pastry base.
7. Cool in the fridge and leave to set for a few hours.

Great on its own, or with some whipped or squirty plant-based cream.
Transfer to an airtight container and store on the side for 3-5 days. You can also freeze the finished tart in a whole tart or as portions. Defrost slowly.

CARBON IMPACT CHECK

Per Serving	kg CO2 eq.	Compared
This Recipe	0.23	
Typical Recipe[25]	0.52	

NOTES:

This is a great way to use up chickpea water that would otherwise go down the drain.

CHOCOLATE MOUSSE

Reduce your waste with something scrummy.

15 mins   2-3 hours   4 servings   Freezable   *Vegan Friendly*

INGREDIENTS

Aquafaba (Chickpea Water) from 1 can of Chickpeas
130g Coconut Cream
3 tbsp Cocoa
4 tbsp White Sugar

METHOD

1. Weigh all of the ingredients in a single bowl.
2. Whisk with a hand mixer for around **10 minutes**, until thick and airy. You can do this by hand but it will take a bit longer.
3. Spoon into ramekins or mug and chill for a few hours.

Dust with a sprinkling of cocoa and enjoy the satisfaction of reduced waste.
Make them up to a day in advance of eating, or freeze in indiviual portions.

CARBON IMPACT CHECK

Per Serving	kg CO2 eq.	Compared
This Recipe	0.09	
Typical Recipe[26]	0.49	

NOTES:

....
....
....

CAKES

TOP TIP This recipe can be made as cupcakes too. Spoon the mix into cake cases instead and bake for 5 mins less.

VICTORIA SPONGE

A classic British cake, reimagined for the modern kitchen.

10 mins   30 mins   8 servings   Freezable   **V** Vegan Friendly

INGREDIENTS

Cake:
410g Plain Flour
200g White Sugar
1½ tsp Bicarbonate of Soda
1 tsp Baking Powder
270g Plant Milk
2 tsp Vanilla Extract
130g Vegetable Oil
1½ tbsp Vinegar
½ tsp Salt

Frosting:
75g Vegetable/Baking Butter (Not Spread)
100g Icing Sugar
75g Fruit Jam

METHOD

1. Pre-heat the oven to **170°C (150°C Fan)**. Lightly grease or line 2x 7-inch/18cm sandwich tins.
2. Weigh all of the ingredients into a single bowl, ending with the vinegar.
3. Mix until just combined.
4. Pour into the tins and bake in the oven for **25-35 minutes**, until an inserted knife/skewer comes out clean and the tops are slightly browned. Cool on a rack.
5. For the frosting, beat the butter until softened. Sift in the icing sugar (if you don't have a sieve, blend the icing sugar instead, and then add to the butter). Mix until smooth.
6. When cooled, use the frosting mix and jam to sandwich the cakes.

Decorate with a dusting of icing sugar and fresh fruit. Transfer to an airtight container and store on the side for 3-5 days. You can also freeze the finished cake or any leftover buttercream frosting.

CARBON IMPACT CHECK

Per Serving	kg CO2 eq.	Compared
This Recipe	0.21	
Typical Recipe[27]	0.47	

NOTES:

TOP TIP It is important to use block butter and 'full fat' cream cheese in the frosting, otherwise it goes runny.

CARROT CAKE

All plant? Even better.

15 mins · 25 mins · 10+ servings · Freezable · V Vegan Friendly

INGREDIENTS

Cake:
270g Plain Flour
120g Light Brown Sugar
3 tsp Baking Powder
½ tsp Salt
150g Plant Milk
60g Vegetable Oil
2½ tsp Lemon Juice
1½ tsp Ground Cinnamon
1 tsp Ground Mixed Spice
180g Carrots

Frosting:
50g Vegetable/Baking Butter (Not Spread)
50g Full Fat Plant-Based Cream Cheese
115g Icing Sugar

METHOD

1. Pre-heat the oven to **180°C (160°C Fan)**. Line a 12-hole muffin tin with cake cases (reuseble are best).
2. Chop the ends off the carrots and grate using a fine grater. If you don't have a grater, you may also blend them, but this may take a few attempts.
3. Weigh all of the ingredients into a single bowl and add the carrot. Stir until combined and fairly smooth.
4. Pour into the cases and bake in the oven for **25-30 minutes**, until an inserted knife/skewer comes out clean and the tops are slightly browned. Cool on a rack.
5. Beat the butter until soft and fluffy, then beat in the cream cheese. Sift in the icing sugar (if you don't have a sieve, blend the icing sugar and then add to the butter instead). Mix until smooth.
6. When cooled, spread the frosting on top of the cakes.

Decorate with a either pecans or walnuts.
Transfer to an airtight container and store on the side for 2-3 days. You can also freeze the finished cake or any leftover frosting.

CARBON IMPACT CHECK

Per Serving	kg CO2 eq.	Compared
This Recipe	0.12	
Typical Recipe[28]	0.51	

NOTES:

....

....

....

TOP TIP You can make this recipe with other nut butters too. Give them a try and enjoy the results.

PEANUT BUTTER CAKE

Something gloopy turned light and fluffy.

10 mins | 30 mins | 10+ servings | Freezable | Vegan Friendly

INGREDIENTS

Cake:
380g Plain Flour
200g White Sugar
200g Peanut Butter (smooth preferred, but crunchy can give a good twist)
1 tsp Salt
2 tsp Bicarbonate of Soda
70g Vegetable Oil
480mL Water
2 tbsp Vinegar

Frosting:
50g Vegetable/Baking Butter (Not Spread)
100g Icing Sugar
50g Peanut Butter

METHOD

1. Pre-heat the oven to **180°C (160°C Fan)**. Lightly grease or line a 23cm/9-inch square baking tin.
2. In a large mixing bowl, mix all of the cake ingredients together until smooth.
3. Pour the mixture into the tin and spread to the edges. Bake in the oven for **30-35 minutes**, until an inserted knife/skewer comes out clean and the tops are slightly browned. Cool on a rack.
4. For the frosting, beat the baking butter until softened. Sift in the icing sugar (if you don't have a sieve, blend the icing sugar and then add to the butter instead). Mix in the peanut butter until smooth.
5. When cooled, spread the frosting on the top of the cake.

Chop into squares and serve. For decoration, you may want to sprinkle some chopped peanuts on top.
Transfer to an airtight container and store on the side for 3-5 days. You can also freeze the finished cake or any leftover buttercream frosting.

CARBON IMPACT CHECK

Per Serving	kg CO2 eq.	Compared
This Recipe	0.16	
Typical Recipe[29]	0.42	

NOTES:

....

....

....

TOP TIP Only want half a cake? Make half the recipe in one tin and then chop the cake in half and stack.

CHOCOLATE CAKE

What cookbook would be complete without one?

10 mins   30 mins   8 servings   Freezable   Vegan Friendly

INGREDIENTS

Cake:
400g Plain Flour
200g White Sugar
150g Cocoa Powder
2 tsp Bicarbonate of Soda
150g Vegetable Oil
500mL Water
220g Plant Milk
2 tbsp Vinegar

Frosting:
120g Vegetable/Baking Butter (Not Spread)
160g Icing Sugar
40g Cocoa Powder
30g Plant Milk

METHOD

1. Pre-heat the oven to **180°C (160°C Fan)**. Lightly grease or line 2x 7-inch/18cm sandwich tins.
2. Weigh all of the cake ingredients into a single bowl, ending with the vinegar. Mix until just combined and smooth.
3. Pour into the tins and bake in the oven for **25-35 minutes**, until an inserted knife/skewer comes out clean. Cool on a rack.
4. Beat the butter and milk together until softened. Sift in the icing sugar and cocoa (if you don't have a sieve, blend the icing sugar instead, and then add to the butter). Mix until smooth.
5. When cooled, use the frosting mix to sandwich and top the cakes.

Good as it is, but for fancy decoration, drizzle melted chocolate on top.
Transfer to an airtight container and store on the side for 3-5 days. You can also freeze the finished cake or any leftover buttercream frosting.

CARBON IMPACT CHECK

Per Serving	kg CO2 eq.	Compared
This Recipe	0.26	
Typical Recipe[30]	0.57	

NOTES:

....

....

....

TOP TIP Like an extra drizzly drizzle cake? Add some bonus lemon juice to the drizzle before you pour on top.

LEMON & LIME DRIZZLE CAKE

Super simple, you can't go wrong!

15 mins   30 mins   8 servings   Freezable   Vegan Friendly

INGREDIENTS

Cake:
275g Plain Flour
3 tsp Baking Powder
150g White Sugar
Zest of 1 Lemon
Zest of 1 Lime
90g Vegetable Oil
150mL Water

Drizzle:
Juice of Lemon and Lime Used In Cake
100g White Sugar

METHOD

1. Pre-heat the oven to **180°C (160°C Fan)**. Lightly grease or line a 20cm loaf tin.
2. Weigh all of the cake ingredients into a single bowl and mix to combine until smooth. Use a small grater instead of a zester if you don't have one.
3. Pour into the tin and bake in the oven for **30-40 minutes**, until an inserted knife/skewer comes out clean and the top is slightly browned.
4. Whilst the loaf cooks, juice the lemon and lime you used earlier. Add the sugar and stir into a runny paste.
5. When the cake comes out of the oven, pierce the top all over with a knife, and pour the drizzle on top. Leave to cool in the tin.

Decorate with some extra zest or enjoy on its own.
Transfer to an airtight container and store on the side for 3-5 days. You can also freeze the finished cake.

CARBON IMPACT CHECK

Per Serving	kg CO2 eq.	Compared
This Recipe	0.13	
Typical Recipe[31]	0.44	

NOTES:

....

....

....

TOP TIP Got a banana on the turn? Put it in a bag in the freezer and defrost when ready to make this cake.

BANANA CAKE

A great way to use bananas which have gone too far!

10 mins 30 mins 8 servings Freezable Vegan Friendly

INGREDIENTS

3 Ripe Bananas
70g Vegetable Oil
75g Light Brown Sugar
225g Plain Flour
3-4 tsp Baking Powder (depending on how dense you want the cake)
2 tsp Cinnamon
1/2 tsp Nutmeg
50g Chocolate Chips or Chopped Nuts

50-100g Peanut Butter (optional)

METHOD

1. Pre-heat the oven to **180°C (160°C Fan)**. Lightly grease or line a 20cm loaf tin.
2. In a large mixing bowl, mash the bananas with a fork or masher, then mix in all of the other cake ingredients (except the peanut butter) until combined.
3. Pour the mixture into the tin. If using the peanut butter, then place in large dollops on top of the batter before baking.
4. Bake for **30-40 mins**, until an inserted knife comes out clean. Allow to cool in the tin for 10 minutes before turning onto a cooling rack.

Serve in slices. If you feel very decadent, try making the frosting from the peanut butter cake and top this cake with it.

Transfer to an airtight container and store on the side for 2-3 days. You can also freeze the finished cake.

CARBON IMPACT CHECK

Per Serving	kg CO2 eq.	Compared
This Recipe	0.13	
Typical Recipe[32]	0.24	

NOTES:

....

....

....

TOP TIP This recipe can really become your own as you can try all sorts of combinations. Keep a note of the best.

FUDGY MUD CAKES

So many options... make them your own.

20 mins   30 mins   10+ servings   Freezable   Vegan Friendly

INGREDIENTS

Cake:
200g Plain Flour
80g Dark Brown Sugar
160g Vegetable/Baking Butter/Spread
2 tsp Baking Powder
1½ tbsp Water
80g Maple Syrup (Golden is also fine)
160g Plant Milk
120g of your choice of chocolate, or any spread of your choosing; e.g. A good combination is 40g Chocolate, 80g Biscuit Spread.

Frosting:
100g Dark Brown Sugar
65g Vegetable/Baking Butter/Spread
½ tsp Salt
40g Plant Milk
100g Icing Sugar

METHOD

1. Pre-heat the oven to **160°C (140°C Fan)**. Line a 12-hole muffin tin with cake cases (reuseble are best).
2. Melt the butter, sugar, water, syrup, milk, and spread/chocolate combination together in a medium-large saucepan over a low-medium heat. Stir until smooth, then remove from the heat and leave to cool for **10 minutes**.
3. After cooling, add the flour and baking powder and mix until smooth.
4. Pour into the cases and bake in the oven for **30-40 minutes**, until an inserted knife/skewer comes out clean. Cool on a rack.
5. In the pan you used earlier, melt the sugar, butter, salt, and milk for the frosting together over a low-medium heat.
6. Slowly increase the heat and bring to the boil for **3 minutes**. Be careful as it may spit and will be very hot.
7. Remove from the heat and whisk in the icing sugar until smooth.
8. Whilst it is still warm, pour on the top of the cakes. Leave to cool.

Transfer to an airtight container and store on the side for 3-5 days. You can also freeze the finished cake or any leftover frosting.

CARBON IMPACT CHECK

Per Serving	kg CO2 eq.	Compared
This Recipe	0.17	
Typical Recipe[33]	0.49	

NOTES:

....

....

....

TOP TIP   Try other dried fruits in place of the dates to give other twists on this recipe.

TOFFEE APPLE CAKE

Fruity and full of fibre whilst treading lightly.

10 mins 50 mins 8 servings Freezable **V** Vegan Friendly

INGREDIENTS

225g Plain Flour
175g Dark Brown Sugar
100g Chopped Dates (dates can be tough to chop - saves a lot of time)
3 tbsp Vegetable Oil
6 tbsp Water or Apple Juice
1 Large Cooking Apple
4 tsp Baking Powder

METHOD

1. Pre-heat the oven to **160°C (140°C Fan)**. Lightly grease or line a 23cm/9-inch square baking tin.
2. Peel (optional) and chop the apple into 0.5cm cubes, discarding the core.
3. Add to a single bowl with the remaining ingredients. Mix until combined.
4. Pour into the tin and bake in the oven for **50-60 minutes**, until an inserted knife/skewer comes out clean and the top has darkened. Cool on a rack.

Serve with a little maple syrup drizzled on top.
Transfer to an airtight container and store on the side for 2-3 days. You can also freeze the finished cake.

CARBON IMPACT CHECK

Per Serving	kg CO2 eq.	Compared
This Recipe	0.14	
Typical Recipe[34]	0.40	

NOTES:

....

....

....

TOP TIP If you want a lighter cake, swap the treacle for more golden syrup instead.

GINGER CAKE

My personal favourite, particularly with a side of custard.

15 mins   20 mins   12 servings   Freezable   *Vegan Friendly*

INGREDIENTS

Cake:
450g Plain Flour
200g Golden Syrup
200g Black Treacle
150g Vegetable Oil
1½ tsp Bicarbonate of Soda
5 tsp Ground Ginger
1 tsp Ground Cinnamon
1 tsp Ground Nutmeg
3 tbsp Plant Milk
½ tsp Salt
330mL Boiling Water

Glaze:
50g Golden Syrup

METHOD

1. Pre-heat the oven to **180°C (160°C Fan)**. Lightly grease or line a 23cm/9-inch square baking tin.
2. Weigh all of the ingredients, except the water, into a single bowl and mix until smooth. The mix will be quite thick.
3. Add the boiling water and mix until smooth again.
4. Pour into the tin and bake in the oven for **20-30 minutes**, until an inserted knife/skewer comes out clean. Cool on a rack.
5. Heat the glaze syrup in a mug in the microwave for 30 seconds, until runny. Be careful as it will get very hot. Spread the syrup over the top of the cake to give it an even shine.

Transfer to an airtight container and store on the side for 3-5 days. You can also freeze the finished cake.

CARBON IMPACT CHECK

Per Serving	kg CO2 eq.	Compared
This Recipe	0.12	
Typical Recipe[35]	0.58	

NOTES:

....

....

....

BISCUITS, COOKIES & TRAYBAKES

TOP TIP | Be careful not to overcook the brownies as they turn from gooey to crispy very quickly.

BROWNIES

Contrary to popular belief, they can be made without eggs.

15 mins   15 mins   9+ servings   Freezable   Vegan Friendly

INGREDIENTS

150g Plain Flour
180g White Sugar
90g Vegetable Oil
80g Plant Milk
75g Cocoa Powder
1 tsp Baking Powder
100g Chocolate
1 tsp Bicarbonate of Soda
½ tsp Salt

METHOD

1. Pre-heat the oven to **170°C (150°C Fan)**. Lightly grease or line a 23cm/9-inch square baking tin.
2. Weigh all of the ingredients, except the chocolate, into a single bowl. Chop 50g of the chocolate into chunks and add to the mixture. Stir well and be prepared for the mixture to be hard going!
3. Melt the remaining 50g of the chocolate in a microwave at 50% power, then mix into the batter.
4. Spread into the tin and bake in the oven for **15-20 minutes**, until an inserted knife/skewer comes out almost clean. Cut whilst warm, and leave to cool on a rack in the tin.

If you are feeling decadent, top with more melted chocolate.
Transfer to an airtight container and store on the side for 3-5 days. You can also freeze spares if needed.

CARBON IMPACT CHECK

Per Serving	kg CO2 eq.	Compared
This Recipe	0.10	
Typical Recipe[36]	0.40	

NOTES:

....

....

....

TOP TIP Try out other cereals in this recipe. Malted wheats are great for Easter nests.

PEANUT CRISPY CAKE

A great one for kids and adults alike.

 5 mins   2-3 hours   15+ servings  Not Freezable Vegan Friendly

INGREDIENTS

200g Peanut Butter
200g Golden Syrup
200g Cornflakes

METHOD

1. Melt the peanut butter and golden syrup in a large saucepan. Be careful not to boil it.
2. Remove from the heat and stir in the cornflakes until well coated.
3. Spread onto a large baking tray and flatten down. Chill for a few hours.

Super simple and takes no time at all to make.
Transfer to an airtight container when set and store on the side for 3-5 days. Sadly, this one can't be frozen.

CARBON IMPACT CHECK

Per Serving	kg CO2 eq.	Compared
This Recipe	0.05	
Typical Recipe[37]	0.10	

NOTES:

....

....

....

TOP TIP There are always bits that crumble off when cutting flapjack. Why not sprinkle them on your breakfast?

FLAPJACK

Super simple, lower impact.

| 10 mins | 20 mins | 12+ servings | Not Freezable | Vegan Friendly |

INGREDIENTS

200g Vegetable/Baking Butter/Spread
225g Golden Syrup
400g Rolled Oats
75g Dried Fruit

METHOD

1. Pre-heat the oven to **180°C (160°C Fan)**. Lightly grease or line a 23cm/9-inch square baking tin.
2. In a large saucepan, melt the butter and golden syrup together.
3. Remove from the heat and add the dried fruit and oats. Stir until well combined.
4. Spread in the prepared tin and bake for **18-25 minutes** until the top has slightly browned. Cool on a rack in the tin.

Great for packed lunches or as a sneaky mid-morning snack.
Transfer to an airtight container and store on the side for up to a week. This one isn't freezable, sorry!

CARBON IMPACT CHECK

Per Serving	kg CO2 eq.	Compared
This Recipe	0.09	
Typical Recipe[38]	0.13	

NOTES:

....

....

....

TOP TIP Prefer a softer cookie? Drop the cooking time by a minute or two to get them how you like.

CHOC-CHUNK COOKIES

Usually gone before they've even cooled.

10 mins   15 mins   8 servings   Freezable   Vegan Friendly

INGREDIENTS

150g Plain Flour
100g White Sugar
100g Vegetable/Baking Butter (Not Spread)
1 tsp Baking Powder
2 tbsp Golden Syrup
100g Chocolate

METHOD

1. Pre-heat the oven to **190°C (170°C Fan)**. Lightly grease or line a large baking tray/ sheet.
2. Cream the butter, sugar, and syrup together until soft and well mixed.
3. Chop the chocolate into chunks and add, with the flour, to the butter mix. Stir until a dough forms.
4. Spoon onto the baking tray and flatten slightly in 8-10 blobs. They do spread a little, so give them space. Don't worry if you don't have room as you can always bake them in a couple of batches.
5. Bake in the oven for **15-20 minutes**, until the edges are slightly browned. Cool on a rack.

Best served with a glass of plant milk in traditional fashion.
Transfer to an airtight container and store on the side for 3-5 days. You can also freeze any leftovers, if you have any!

CARBON IMPACT CHECK

Per Serving	kg CO2 eq.	Compared
This Recipe	0.11	
Typical Recipe[39]	0.20	

NOTES:

....

....

....

TOP TIP Make sure to give plenty of room around each cookie when baking as they tend to spread.

OATMEAL & RAISIN COOKIES

An underrated flavour; will you agree?

10 mins 15 mins 8 servings Freezable Vegan Friendly

INGREDIENTS

115g Plain Flour
140g Rolled Oats
40g Plant Milk
35g White Sugar
25g Brown Sugar
65g Vegetable/Baking Butter (Not Spread)
75g Raisins
½ tsp Bicarbonate of Soda
1 tsp Ground Cinnamon

METHOD

1. Pre-heat the oven to **190°C (170°C Fan)** Lightly grease or line a large baking tray/sheet.
2. Cream the butter, sugars, and milk together until soft and well mixed.
3. Add the remaining ingredients and stir until a dough forms.
4. Spoon onto the baking tray and flatten slightly in 8-10 blobs. They do spread a little, so give them space. Don't worry if you don't have room as you can always bake them in a couple of batches.
5. Bake in the oven for **15-20 minutes**, until the edges are slightly browned. Cool on a rack.

Try these in a taste-off with the chocolate chunk cookies on the previous page.
Transfer to an airtight container and store on the side for 3-5 days. You can also freeze any leftovers, if you have any!

CARBON IMPACT CHECK

Per Serving	kg CO2 eq.	Compared
This Recipe	0.09	
Typical Recipe[40]	0.13	

NOTES:

....
....
....

TOP TIP Swap out the golden syrup for maple syrup or treacle for a very different biscuit.

OATY BISCUITS

Like a well-known brand, but better because you made them.

| 10 mins | 15 mins | 10+ servings | Freezable | Vegan Friendly |

INGREDIENTS

115g Plain Flour
100g White Sugar
115g Rolled Oats
115g Vegetable/Baking Butter/Spread
1 tbsp Golden Syrup
½ tsp Bicarbonate of Soda
2 tsp Water

METHOD

1. Pre-heat the oven to **180°C (160°C Fan)**. Lightly grease or line a large baking tray/ sheet.
2. In a large saucepan, melt the butter with the sugar, syrup, and water.
3. Remove from the heat and add the remaining ingredients and mix until well combined.
4. Spoon onto the baking tray and flatten slightly in 10+ blobs, depending on how big you'd like them. They don't spread far, so don't need much space around them. Don't worry if you don't have room as you can always bake them in a couple of batches.
5. Bake in the oven for **10-15 minutes**, until the edges are slightly browned. Cool on a rack.

These biscuits go very well with a hot chocolate.
Transfer to an airtight container and store on the side for 3-5 days. You can also freeze any leftovers, if you have any!

CARBON IMPACT CHECK

Per Serving	kg CO2 eq.	Compared
This Recipe	0.07	
Typical Recipe[41]	0.10	

NOTES:

....

....

....

TOP TIP: The snap in these biscuits will only come if they're thin and are cooked for long enough. Be careful!

GINGER NUTS

Spicy to the taste with a good snap.

10 mins | 15 mins | 12+ servings | Freezable | Vegan Friendly

INGREDIENTS

200g Plain Flour
100g White Sugar
100g Vegetable/Baking Butter (Not Spread)
½ tsp Bicarbonate of Soda
1 tbsp Ground Ginger
75g Golden Syrup

METHOD

1. Pre-heat the oven to **190°C (170°C Fan)**. Lightly grease or line a large baking tray/sheet.
2. Cream the butter, sugar, and syrup together until soft and well mixed.
3. Add the remaining ingredients and stir until a dough forms.
4. Spoon onto the baking tray and flatten slightly in 12+ blobs. They do spread a little, so give them space to spread. Don't worry if you don't have room as you can always bake them in a couple of batches.
5. Bake in the oven for **15-20 minutes**, until the edges are slightly browned. Cool on a rack.

Best served dunked in a cup of tea in the afternoon.
Transfer to an airtight container and store on the side for 3-5 days. You can also freeze any leftovers, if you have any!

CARBON IMPACT CHECK

Per Serving	kg CO2 eq.	Compared
This Recipe	0.06	
Typical Recipe[42]	0.08	

NOTES:

TOP TIP

A great flavour combination to try is chocolate and cranberry. What's your favourite?

SHORTBREAD

Buttery goodness gone plant-based.

10 mins   15 mins   6 servings   Freezable   Vegan Friendly

INGREDIENTS

250g Plain Flour
150g Vegetable/Baking Butter (Not Spread)
75g White Sugar
50-75g Extras (e.g. cocolate chunks, fruit)

METHOD

1. Pre-heat the oven to **180°C (160°C Fan)**. Lightly grease or line a 7-inch/18cm sandwich tin.
2. Weigh all of the ingredients into a single bowl and mix until a dough forms.
3. Squash the dough into the baking tin using your hands. Make sure to flatten right to the edges.
4. Bake for **15-20 minutes**, until the edges start to brown. Cut the pieces in the tin whilst hot, and then leave to cool in the tin on a rack.

Transfer to an airtight container and store on the side for 3-5 days. You can also freeze the pieces individually. Give them a few minutes in the oven when defrosting if you want to crisp them up again.

CARBON IMPACT CHECK

Per Serving	kg CO2 eq.	Compared
This Recipe	0.15	
Typical Recipe[43]	0.19	

NOTES:

....

....

....

TOP TIP If your cream won't stay thick, try adding a little cornflour to stabilise it.

SCONES

Cream then jam, or jam then cream... that's the question.

10 mins   15 mins   8+ servings   Freezable   Vegan Friendly

INGREDIENTS

335g Plain Flour
3 tsp Baking Powder
25g White Sugar
100g Vegetable/Baking Butter/Spread
150g Sultanas
165g Plant Milk (keep 15g separate)
1 tsp Golden Syrup/Maple Syrup/Agave Nectar

METHOD

1. Pre-heat the oven to **210°C (190°C Fan)** Lightly grease or line a large baking sheet.
2. Except for the milk and syrup, rub all of the ingredients together into a single bowl until it resembles breadcrumbs.
3. Add 150ml of the milk gradually, and mix until a dough forms. You may not need all of the milk.
4. Roll the dough out on a floured surface, until it is about 1.5-2cm thick (think 1-2 burgers thick). Flatten with your hands if you don't have a rolling pin.
5. Using a biscuit cutter (5-10cm in size), cut the scones out of the dough. If you don't have a cutter, use an upturned glass, mug, or jar.
6. Mix the remaining milk and syrup together and brush on the top of the scones. Bake for **15-20 minutes**, until golden on top. Cool on a rack.

Serve with some jam and whipped plant-based cream (double will work best).
Transfer to an airtight container and store on the side for 2-3 days. You can also freeze the finished scones as needed.

CARBON IMPACT CHECK

Per Serving	kg CO2 eq.	Compared
This Recipe	0.15	
Typical Recipe[44]	0.19	

NOTES:

CALCULATIONS

The carbon comparisons on each page have been carefully calculated around a set of assumptions. As a researcher, it only seems right to share these with you. Not everyone will be interested in this bit, but it is here if you are...

The main source of information is the Vegan Society's Plate Up For The Planet Carbon Calculator[45]. This is a great source of data on emissions associated with your food. Where this has been used, a reasonable assumption of where the food has originated has been made, guided by some of the suggestions from "How Bad Are Bananas?"[46].

Where foodstuffs are not listed on the Vegan Society's Plate Up For The Planet database[45], I have used information provided by some manufacturers (e.g. Oatly list the emissions of each product on their packaging), other smaller carbon databases, or individual studies/websites.

Armed with this information, I have added the associated emissions for the ingredients of each recipe in this book to create a per serving impact. In a similar way, I have then repeated the exercise for a popular "typical" recipe from the internet. This comparator is likely from a celebrity chef, or well known recipe site.

Now, there is a lot more to the emissions of your food than just the ingredients, including cooking energy, transportation from the supermarket, etc; however, the key changes in these recipes are the ingredients, so the comparison is still a good indicator of the improvement.

All of the sources and comparison recipes are given on the next page, should you wish to check my numbers!

You may also want to consider the water usage, land take-up, and ethics of your food. Sounds like a lot of effort, right? Support the movement for better labelling of foods so you can make better decisions more easily.

REFERENCES

1-44 are the comparator recipes. All of the links below were last accessed in December 2021.
1. Leek and Potato Soup | https://www.bbcgoodfood.com/recipes/leek-potato-soup
2. Basic Shortcrust Pastry | https://www.bbcgoodfood.com/recipes/basic-shortcrust-pastry
3. Chicken and Mushroom Pie | https://www.bbc.co.uk/food/recipes/chickenandmushroompi_89034
4. Quiche Recipe | https://sallysbakingaddiction.com/quiche-recipe/
5. Savoury Mince Crumble | https://realfood.tesco.com/recipes/savoury-mince-crumble.html
6. Cottage Pie | https://www.recipetineats.com/cottage-pie/
7. Chicken Jallof Rice | https://tasty.co/recipe/chicken-jollof-rice
8. Chilli Con-Carne | https://www.bbcgoodfood.com/recipes/chilli-con-carne-recipe
9. Contest Winning Peanut Chicken Stir Fry | https://www.tasteofhome.com/recipes/contest-winning-peanut-chicken-stir-fry/
10. Chicken Noodle Soup | https://www.bbcgoodfood.com/recipes/chicken-noodle-soup
11. Thai Green Chicken Curry | https://www.bbcgoodfood.com/recipes/thai-green-chicken-curry
12. 15-Minute Indian Curry with Chicken and Peas | https://www.foodnetwork.com/recipes/food-network-kitchen/15-minute-indian-curry-with-chicken-and-peas-3676442
13. Easy Chicken and Pea Risotto | https://www.bbc.co.uk/food/recipes/easy_chicken_and_pea_31687
14. Ultimate Spaghetti Carbonara Recipe | https://www.bbcgoodfood.com/recipes/ultimate-spaghetti-carbonara-recipe
15. Pasta with Meatballs | https://realfood.tesco.com/recipes/pasta-with-meatballs.html
16. Simple Lasagne | https://realfood.tesco.com/recipes/simple-lasagne.html
17. Classic Homemade Burger | https://realfood.tesco.com/recipes/classic-homemade-burger.html
18. Meatloaf Recipe | https://www.recipetineats.com/meatloaf-recipe/
19. Apple Crumble with Custard | https://realfood.tesco.com/recipes/apple-crumble-with-custard.html
20. Apple and Blackberry Pie | https://www.deliaonline.com/recipes/seasons/what-should-you-be-cooking-in-august/apple-and-blackberry-pie
21. Mary's Sticky Toffee Pudding | https://www.bbc.co.uk/food/recipes/marys_sticky_toffee_41970
22. Chocolate Lava Cake | https://www.bbc.co.uk/food/recipes/chocolate_lava_cake_79464
23. Berry Pudding | https://www.taste.com.au/recipes/berry-pudding/ee368824-dcad-4aba-a203-22c0ff918016
24. Apple & Strawberry Crumble Cake | https://www.taste.com.au/recipes/apple-strawberry-crumble-cake/505ce333-05ce-4fc6-b956-e5579679c01e
25. Old School Butterscotch Tart | https://flawlessfood.co.uk/old-school-butterscotch-tart/
26. Chocolate Mousse | https://www.recipetineats.com/chocolate-mousse/
27. Victoria Sponge Cake | https://realfood.tesco.com/recipes/victoria-sponge-cake.html
28. Carrot Cake | https://www.bbcgoodfood.com/recipes/carrot-cake
29. Killer Peanut Butter Cake | https://www.daringgourmet.com/killer-peanut-butter-cake/
30. Easy Chocolate Cake | https://www.bbcgoodfood.com/recipes/easy-chocolate-cake
31. Lemon Drizzle Cake | https://www.bbcgoodfood.com/recipes/lemon-drizzle-cake
32. Banana Bread | https://www.simplyrecipes.com/recipes/banana_bread/
33. Caramel Mud Cake | https://www.taste.com.au/recipes/caramel-mud-cake/ba48c9c7-9821-44e0-a336-8ce0e1488b9f
34. Toffee Apple Cake | https://www.sainsburysmagazine.co.uk/recipes/cakes/toffee-apple-cake
35. Jamaican Ginger Cake | https://realfood.tesco.com/recipes/jamaican-ginger-cake.html
36. Easy Chocolate Brownies | https://www.recipetineats.com/easy-chocolate-brownies/#wprm-recipe-container-24736
37. Chocolate Rice Crispy Cakes | https://realfood.tesco.com/recipes/chocolate-rice-crispy-cakes.html
38. Yummy Golden Syrup Flapjacks | https://www.bbcgoodfood.com/recipes/yummy-golden-syrup-flapjacks
39. The Best Chewy Chocolate Chip Cookies | https://tasty.co/recipe/the-best-chewy-chocolate-chip-cookies
40. Gemma's Best-Ever Oatmeal Cookies | https://www.biggerbolderbaking.com/oatmeal-cookies-best-ever/
41. Oat Biscuits | https://www.bbcgoodfood.com/recipes/oat-biscuits-0
42. Ginger Biscuits | https://www.bbcgoodfood.com/recipes/ginger-biscuits
43. Classic Shortbread | https://realfood.tesco.com/recipes/classic-shortbread.html
44. Classic Scones with Jam and Clotted Cream | https://www.bbcgoodfood.com/recipes/classic-scones-jam-clotted-cream
45. Vegan Society Plate Up For The Planet Carbon Calculator | Harwatt, H., Small World Consulting, Blueberry Consultants | https://assets.plateupfortheplanet.org/carbon-calculator/
46. How bad are bananas? The carbon footprint of everything. | Berners-Lee, M. (2010)
47. Differences in Environmental Impact between Plant-Based Alternatives to Dairy and Dairy Products: A Systematic Literature Review | Carlsson Kanyama, A.; Hedin, B.; Katzeff, C. | 2021 | https://doi.org/10.3390/su132212599
48. Health Environment Animals Laborers Label - Food Ingredient Guide | https://healabel.com/ingredient-guide
49. OpenCO2 Emission Factor Database | https://www.openco2.net/en/search-emission-factors
50. Environmental analysis along the supply chain of dark, milk and white chocolate: a life cycle comparison | Bianchi, F.R., Moreschi, L., Gallo, M. et al. | 2020 | https://doi.org/10.1007/s11367-020-01817-6
51. A life cycle assessment of Agaricus bisporus mushroom production in the USA | Robinson, B., Winans, K., Kendall, A. et al. | 2018 | https://doi.org/10.1007/s11367-018-1456-6
52. The greenhouse gas footprint of Booths | Small World Consulting Ltd. | 2015 | https://www.booths.co.uk/wp-content/uploads/Booths-GHG-Report-2014.pdf
53. Carbon Cloud Climate Hub | https://apps.carboncloud.com/climatehub/
54. Violife Sustainability | https://violifefoods.com/sustainability/
55. National Geographic - Sustainable Shopping - Which Bag Is Best? | https://www.nationalgeographic.org/media/sustainable-shoppingwhich-bag-best/

OTHER ECO TIPS

...to save the planet and your wallet.

This isn't a page where I just rant about things you probably already know about (e.g. drive less, use public transport more, etc.). It is more a case of making you think bigger.

Everywhere you look, there is 'green-washing' going on and it is very difficult to know what is right.
Take plastic bags for example, they are now replaced with paper bags which is great for the oceans, but need using many more times than a plastic bag to balance the energy and emissions[55].

The best thing you can do to reduce your impact is to simply not waste. The bag that wins is the fabric one that is used over and over until it falls apart.

Apply this in every case you can...
Buy and cook only what you need or can store.
Use non-disposable, re-usable alternatives to clingfilm and foil.
Use leftover bread and cereal bags to wrap foods.
Try not to fly, but if you do then make the most of your trip and do something worthwhile.
Buy used instead of new. Chances are it is much cheaper too.

There are many more, but I would need more than this page to list them. Just try to remember this when you go about your day to day life, and try to stick to your principles.

Making any effort is better than doing nothing, and if you can encourage a friend to do the same as well, then even better.

ABOUT THE AUTHOR

Andy Oakey

Andy Oakey developed his interest in sustainable eating after going plant-based in 2019. The COVID-19 lockdown inspired him to experiment with recipes to make plant-based eating less difficult and intimidating. Fitting recipe development around a busy lifestyle as a full-time researcher and triathlete, Andy is working to help others to reduce their impact.

He made his on stage debut at the Bournemouth Foodies Festival in 2021. Look out for him at future events to see him demonstrate live.